This journal belongs to

_____
_____
_____
_____

ALSO BY K. A. LAST

Fiction

Sacrifice – A Fall For Me Prequel
(The Tate Chronicles, #0.5)

Bound (The Tate Chronicles, #0.6)

Fall For Me (The Tate Chronicles, #1)

Fight For Me (The Tate Chronicles, #2)

Die For Me (The Tate Chronicles, #3)

The Tate Chronicles Omnibus

Immagica

The Lovely Dark

Something (All the Things: part one)

Nothing (All the Things: part two)

Everything (All the Things: part three)

The Other Side of Me (All the Things: part four)

All the Things (Something, Nothing, Everything)

Non-fiction

The Tate Chronicles Notebook

Immagica Notebook

A Novel Idea! Colouring Journal for Writers

A Novel IDEA

Workbook for Writers

K. A. LAST

Copyright © 2019 K. A. Last. All rights reserved.

First published in Australia 2019 by K. A. Last

The right of K. A. Last to be identified as the author of this work has been asserted by her under the *Copyright Amendment (Moral Rights) Act 2000*.

This work is copyright. Apart from any use as permitted under the *Copyright Act 1968*, no part of this publication may be reproduced, stored in a retrieval system, recorded or transmitted in any form or by any means, electronic, mechanical, photocopying, recording or otherwise, without the prior written permission of the publisher.

K. A. Last
kalast@kalastbooks.com.au
www.kalastbooks.com.au

ISBN: 978-0-6480257-6-4

Set in Bookman Old Style 10pt

Formatting and cover design © KILA Designs
www.kiladesigns.com.au | www.facebook.com/KILAdesigns

Edited by Lauren Clarke | www.creatingink.com

*For every writer who ever
thought they couldn't,
because your words matter.*

CONTENTS

Introduction	1
AUDITIONS: Let the show begin	**3**
Think about it: Your light bulb moment	4
Name it: Christening your story	10
ACT I: Writing the script	**11**
Frame it: Create your story outline	12
Expand it: Detail your plot	21
Map it: Visualise your story	33
Revise it: Revisit your initial outline	38
ACT II: Casting the characters	**45**
Meet them: Get acquainted with your cast	46
Talk to them: Listen to your characters	62
Dress them: Style your characters	67
ACT III: Setting the stage	**83**
Build it: Design your set	84
DRESS REHEARSAL: The final run-through	**101**
Detail it: Outline your scenes or chapters	102
Develop it: Further ideas	127

INTRODUCTION

As a writer, I often find it hard to get the thoughts in my head straight, and in any sort of coherent order. There are so many voices in there vying for my attention, and at times it feels like one big jumbled mess. Over the years I've tried different things, including pantsing and plotting my stories, and I've come to realise that for me, the best and most productive method is outlining my ideas in detail first. Once I have a solid outline, I find that when I sit down to write I waste less time, because I already know what I want to write about.

But getting to the point where I have a solid story idea isn't always easy. That's where *A Novel Idea* comes in. I created this workbook to help writers of all ages and skill levels—to help you be as prepared as you can be when you sit down to write.

A Novel Idea is divided into sections, much like the traditional three-act structure of a story plot, but with extra scenes. This workbook will help you develop your story idea from the initial light bulb moment, to all the details about your characters, to visions for the world you want to create.

By the time you finish going through these prompts and exercises, you will have a wonderful story idea to start writing, and a host of invaluable information to refer back to once your first draft is completed. There are no restrictions when it comes to using this workbook. You can complete the sections in order, or if your mind has other ideas feel free to start in the middle, or anywhere else. There is no right or wrong way to go about your creative process.

I wish you every joy and success in your writing, and I hope that *A Novel Idea* will help you create the story you want to tell.

K. A. Last – March 2019

novel • *n.* fictitious prose story of book length.
• *adj.* of new kind or nature; strange; previously unknown.
idea *n.* plan etc. formed by mental effort;
mental impression or concept; vague belief or fancy;
intention, purpose.
– Australian Oxford mini dictionary 4th ed.

And, as imagination bodies forth
The forms of things unknown, the poet's pen
Turns them to shapes, and gives to airy nothing
A local habitation and a name.
William Shakespeare
– A Midsummer Night's Dream, Act V, Scene I

AUDITIONS
Let the show begin

THINK ABOUT IT
Your lightbulb moment

If you're anything like me, you have an overactive mind that's so full of ideas and thoughts you don't know what to do with them. The light bulb in my brain constantly clicks on and off, and if you're reading this, then I bet yours does, too. But what do you do when you've had one of those *click* moments, and you need to get it out of your head before it disappears into the ether? You write it down. Use the following pages to get your ideas onto paper. Don't think about it too much. For now, all you need to do is free up some mental space so you can tackle the details with a clearer mind.

_____

_____

_____

_____

_____

_____

_____

_____

_____

_____

_____

_____

_____

NAME IT
Christening your story

Use this page to brainstorm title ideas. The title of your story may be something that comes to you first, or you might not know what you'd like to name it until you've fleshed out your idea. If that's the case, don't worry—you can come back here at any time to record your thoughts.

_____
_____
_____
_____
_____
_____
_____
_____
_____
_____
_____
_____
_____
_____
_____
_____
_____
_____
_____

ACT I
Writing the script

FRAME IT
Create your story outline

Now it's time to get your initial thoughts working harder for you and write a loose summary of your story. You'll be amazed at how much this will help to get you on track with your ideas. Start by thinking about three things: your main character's goal, motivation, and conflict.

Goal:

_____
_____
_____
_____

Motivation:

_____
_____
_____
_____

Conflict:

_____
_____
_____
_____

Next, have a go at summing up your story in one sentence. This is simply a broad description, and should include your main ideas. For example, the Disney movie, *Tangled*, would go something like this: *A princess with magical hair is kidnapped by a witch, locked in a tower and forced to keep the witch young and beautiful, until an unlikely hero comes to save the princess.* This sentence has identified the key characters, what those characters are up against, and the final outcome. Now try it with your story idea.

_____
_____
_____
_____
_____
_____
_____
_____

The next step is to add more detail to your one-sentence summary. Think about what the main plot points of your story are, and refer to the graph to see where they should roughly fall.

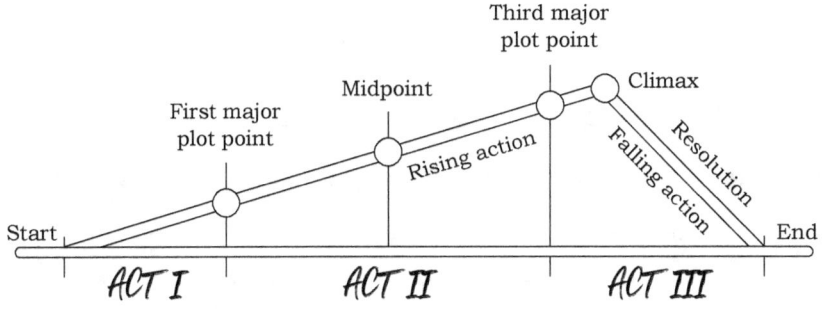

I like to think of each plot point as an event or disaster that my characters must react to or overcome. With this in mind, write a summary paragraph using the following scaffold:

Sentence one: Set up the story.

_____
_____
_____
_____
_____
_____
_____
_____

Sentence two: The first major plot point or the climax of Act I.

_____
_____
_____
_____
_____
_____
_____
_____

Sentence three: The second major plot point or the midpoint.

_____
_____
_____

Sentence four: The third major plot point or the climax of Act II.

Sentence five: Final climax and resolution of the story.

To build your story into an **outline** a few pages long, use the sentences from your summary on the previous pages as a guide to write a couple of paragraphs per sentence.

_____
_____
_____
_____
_____
_____
_____
_____
_____
_____
_____
_____
_____
_____
_____
_____
_____
_____
_____
_____
_____
_____
_____
_____
_____
_____
_____
_____

EXPAND IT
Detail your plot

Now is when you ask yourself: Do I *really* know what my story is about? After completing the **Frame it: Create your story outline** section, you should have a pretty good idea. Use the following pages to expand your loose outline in more detail.

Identify the details of the **main conflict** within your story.

_____
_____
_____
_____
_____
_____
_____
_____
_____
_____
_____
_____
_____
_____
_____
_____
_____
_____
_____
_____
_____
_____

Develop your **first major plot point** and any details of the inciting incident(s) that lead up to it.

Expand on your **second major plot point** and any obstacles your characters might face before and after it occurs.

Build your **third major plot point** and think about how it will lead into the climax of your story.

What is the **climax** of your story? When and how does the **main conflict** reach its deciding moment?

Bring your story to some sort of **resolution** and tie up any loose ends.

At this point you should have a great outline for your story, but if you have **more thoughts**, or you ran out of room, use the following pages to keep writing.

_____
_____
_____
_____
_____
_____
_____
_____
_____
_____
_____
_____
_____
_____
_____
_____
_____
_____
_____
_____
_____
_____
_____
_____
_____
_____
_____

Now that you have an expanded outline for your story, ask yourself if there are any **plot holes** you can foresee? Are there any subplots you'd like to include? Anything you think you've missed? Write about them here.

MAP IT
Visualise your story

Are you a visual person, like me? I often find it helpful to have my ideas laid out in front of me, so I can see them easily at a glance. Whether it's using Post-it notes on a wall, or scribbling on a piece of paper, creating a mind map can be a useful exercise. It can help us see things we may have missed. Once you've written down the basics for your outline and plot structure, maybe it will help to also mind map your story idea. Use the maps on the following pages to help you get your head around the major plot points of your story. It's also a good way to see how any subplots might work with the main plot. You can create your own mind maps on the blank pages, or use the space for anything else you want to record.

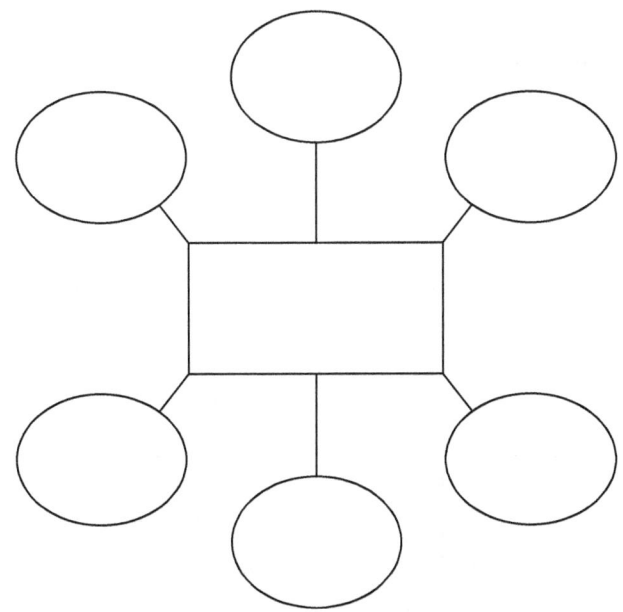

MIND MAP

MIND MAP

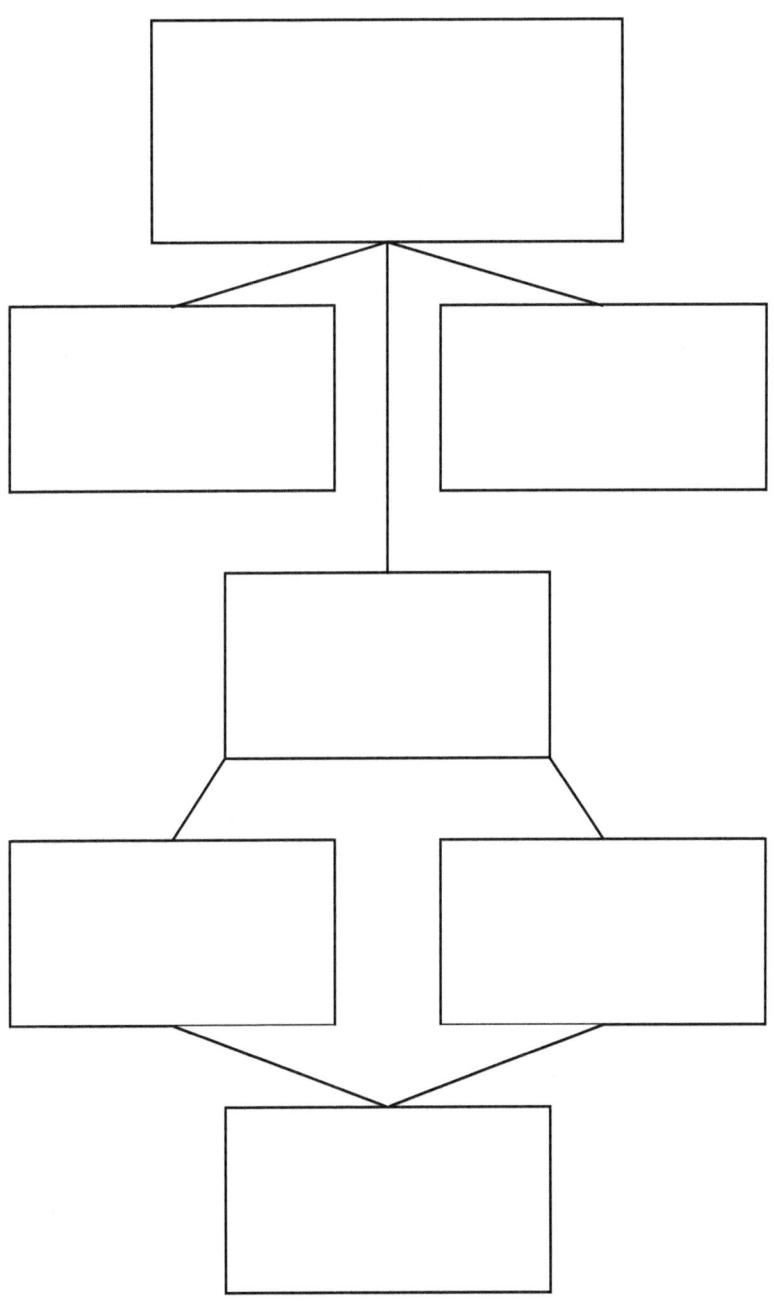

MIND MAP

MIND MAP

REVISE IT
Revisit your initial outline

At this point, you might want to start drafting your story. That's great, but keep in mind that once you've finished your first draft, you should come back here and revise your initial outline. This will help you later when it's time to write your elevator pitch, synopsis, and promotional copy.

One sentence:

_____
_____
_____

One paragraph:

_____
_____
_____
_____
_____
_____
_____
_____
_____
_____

A few pages:

To test your story idea, ask yourself, **why is it exciting?** Record your thoughts in the space below.

ACT II
Casting the characters

MEET THEM
Get acquainted with your cast

You can't tell a story without someone to act it out. Characters are one of the most important aspects of your story, and they need to be fleshed out as much as possible. You should aim to get to know them really well before you start writing so you know how they will react in certain situations, and to the events of your plot. I like to think of my characters as real people, and I try to make them as authentic and believable as possible. Use the following pages to get to know your characters as much as you can. There's space for your protagonist, antagonist, and other secondary characters. From your main star to your stage-hands, take the time to get acquainted with your complete cast. If you like, you can use the space on this page to brainstorm name ideas first, or write down anything else you think will be useful.

Protagonist:

_____
_____
_____
_____
_____
_____
_____
_____

Antagonist:

_____
_____
_____
_____
_____
_____
_____
_____

Secondary characters:

_____
_____
_____
_____
_____
_____
_____
_____
_____
_____
_____
_____
_____
_____
_____
_____
_____

PROTAGONIST PROFILE

Name: _____

_____

Name meaning: _____

_____

_____

Gender: _____

Age: _____

Star sign: _____

Nationality: _____

Height: _____

Weight: _____

Body type: _____

Complexion: _____

Eye colour: _____

Hair colour: _____

Clothing: _____

_____

Career: _____

_____

Demeanour: _____

_____

Speaking manner: _____

_____

Prejudices: _____

_____

Weaknesses: _____

_____

Place photo here

Strengths: _____

_____

_____

Hobbies: _____

_____

Talents: _____

_____

Weapon of choice: _____

Describe your character in one word: _____

Write a short biography: _____

_____

_____

_____

_____

_____

_____

What is your character's ultimate goal? _____

_____

_____

_____

What does your character think they want in comparison to what they really want or need? _____

_____

_____

_____

_____

_____

_____

ANTAGONIST PROFILE

Name: _____

Name meaning: _____
_____
_____

Gender: _____

Age: _____

Star sign: _____

Nationality: _____

Height: _____

Weight: _____

Body type: _____

Complexion: _____

Eye colour: _____

Hair colour: _____

Clothing: _____
_____

Career: _____
_____

Demeanour: _____
_____

Speaking manner: _____
_____

Prejudices: _____
_____

Weaknesses: _____
_____

Place photo here

Strengths: _____

_____

_____

Hobbies: _____

_____

Talents: _____

_____

Weapon of choice: _____

Describe your character in one word: _____

Write a short biography: _____

_____

_____

_____

_____

_____

_____

What is your character's ultimate goal? _____

_____

_____

_____

What does your character think they want in comparison to what they really want or need? _____

_____

_____

_____

_____

_____

_____

CHARACTER PROFILE

Name: _____

Name meaning: _____
_____
_____

Gender: _____

Age: _____

Star sign: _____

Nationality: _____

Height: _____

Weight: _____

Body type: _____

Complexion: _____

Eye colour: _____

Hair colour: _____

Clothing: _____
_____

Career: _____
_____

Demeanour: _____
_____

Speaking manner: _____
_____

Prejudices: _____
_____

Weaknesses: _____
_____

Place photo here

Strengths: _____
_____
_____

Hobbies: _____
_____

Talents: _____
_____

Weapon of choice: _____
Describe your character in one word: _____
Write a short biography: _____
_____
_____
_____
_____
_____

What is your character's ultimate goal? ____
_____
_____

What does your character think they want in comparison to what they really want or need? _____
_____
_____
_____
_____
_____

CHARACTER PROFILE

Name: _____

Name meaning: _____

Gender: _____

Age: _____

Star sign: _____

Nationality: _____

Height: _____

Weight: _____

Body type: _____

Complexion: _____

Eye colour: _____

Hair colour: _____

Clothing: _____

Career: _____

Demeanour: _____

Speaking manner: _____

Prejudices: _____

Weaknesses: _____

Place photo here

Strengths: _____
_____
_____

Hobbies: _____
_____

Talents: _____
_____

Weapon of choice: _____
Describe your character in one word: _____
Write a short biography: _____
_____
_____
_____
_____
_____

What is your character's ultimate goal? _____
_____
_____
_____

What does your character think they want in comparison to what they really want or need? _____
_____
_____
_____
_____
_____
_____

CHARACTER PROFILE

Name: _____

Name meaning: _____
_____
_____

Gender: _____

Age: _____

Star sign: _____

Nationality: _____

Height: _____

Weight: _____

Body type: _____

Complexion: _____

Eye colour: _____

Hair colour: _____

Clothing: _____
_____

Career: _____
_____

Demeanour: _____
_____

Speaking manner: _____
_____

Prejudices: _____
_____

Weaknesses: _____
_____

Place photo here

Strengths: _____

_____

_____

Hobbies: _____

_____

Talents: _____

_____

Weapon of choice: _____

Describe your character in one word: _____

Write a short biography: _____

_____

_____

_____

_____

_____

_____

What is your character's ultimate goal? _____

_____

_____

_____

What does your character think they want in comparison to what they really want or need? _____

_____

_____

_____

_____

_____

CHARACTER PROFILE

Name: _____

Name meaning: _____
_____
_____

Gender: _____

Age: _____

Star sign: _____

Nationality: _____

Height: _____

Weight: _____

Body type: _____

Complexion: _____

Eye colour: _____

Hair colour: _____

Clothing: _____
_____

Career: _____
_____

Demeanour: _____
_____

Speaking manner: _____
_____

Prejudices: _____
_____

Weaknesses: _____
_____

Place photo here

Strengths: _____
_____

Hobbies: _____
_____

Talents: _____
_____

Weapon of choice: _____
Describe your character in one word: _____
Write a short biography: _____
_____
_____
_____
_____
_____
_____

What is your character's ultimate goal? _____
_____
_____
_____

What does your character think they want in comparison to what they really want or need? _____
_____
_____
_____
_____
_____
_____

CHARACTER PROFILE

Name: _____

Name meaning: _____

Gender: _____

Age: _____

Place photo here

Star sign: _____

Nationality: _____

Height: _____

Weight: _____

Body type: _____

Complexion: _____

Eye colour: _____

Hair colour: _____

Clothing: _____

Career: _____

Demeanour: _____

Speaking manner: _____

Prejudices: _____

Weaknesses: _____

Strengths: _____
_____
_____

Hobbies: _____
_____

Talents: _____
_____

Weapon of choice: _____
Describe your character in one word: _____
Write a short biography: _____
_____
_____
_____
_____
_____

What is your character's ultimate goal? _____
_____
_____
_____

What does your character think they want in comparison to what they really want or need?_____
_____
_____
_____
_____
_____

TALK TO THEM
Listen to your characters

My head is constantly full of conversations that I not only have with my characters, but that they have with themselves and each other. I'm always imagining scenes playing out in my head like a movie, and I find it helpful to write down my imagined conversations and interactions. Use the next few pages to record anything you think you may be able to use in your first draft. The key is to be able to come back here for snippets of information your characters may have told you during your initial thought process.

DRESS THEM
Style your characters

Every leading lady or man needs to have their own style. Use this page to brainstorm ideas about your characters' basic dress code, then use the figures on the following pages to sketch ideas for what your main characters would wear. If you're not comfortable with drawing, why not cut out images from magazines and create a vision board for your characters? You can include anything and everything, from shoes, to makeup, to hairstyles. There's also an extra page for anything else that inspires you.

_____
_____
_____
_____
_____
_____
_____
_____
_____
_____
_____
_____
_____
_____
_____
_____
_____

FEMALE PROTAGONIST
Style guide

FEMALE PROTAGONIST
Vision board

MALE PROTAGONIST
Style guide

MALE PROTAGONIST
Vision board

FEMALE ANTAGONIST
Style guide

FEMALE ANTAGONIST
Vision board

MALE ANTAGONIST
Style guide

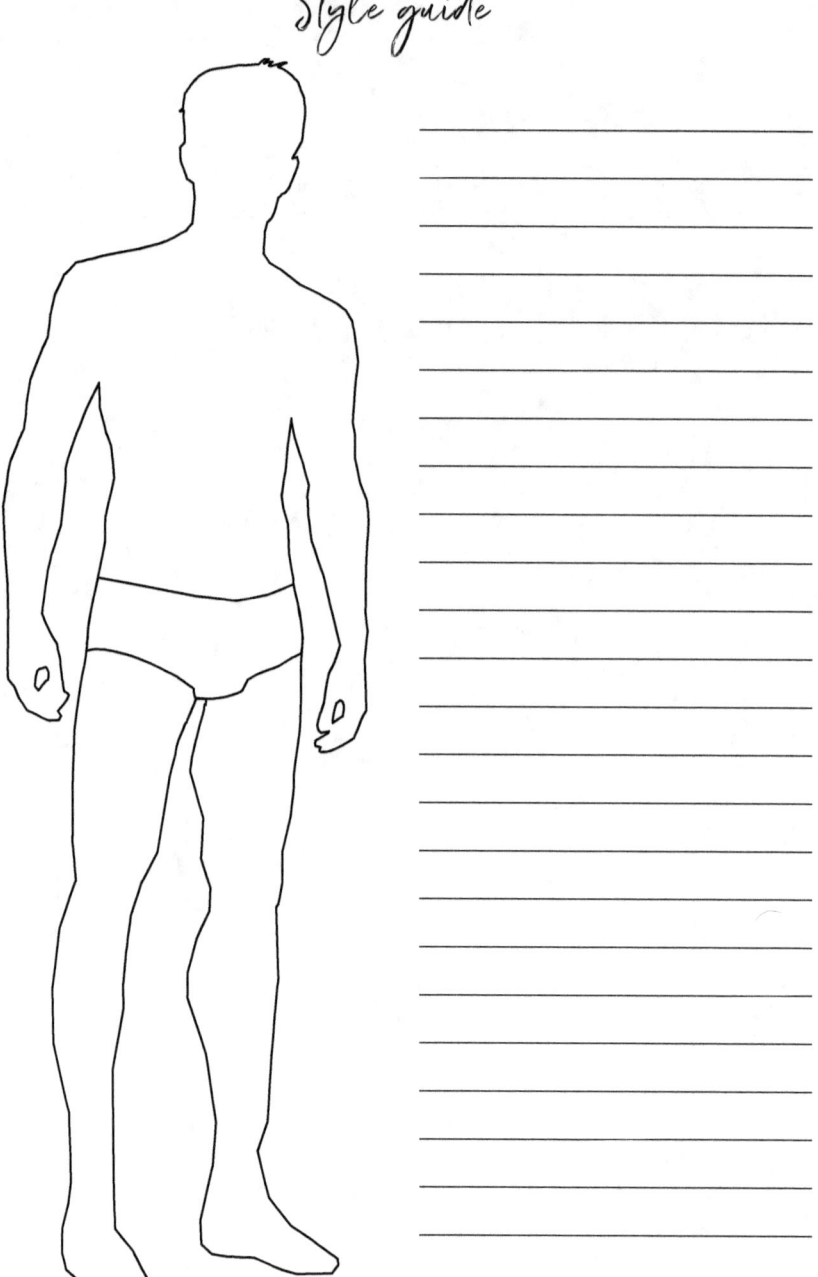

MALE ANTAGONIST
Vision board

FEMALE CHARACTER
Style guide

MALE CHARACTER
Style guide

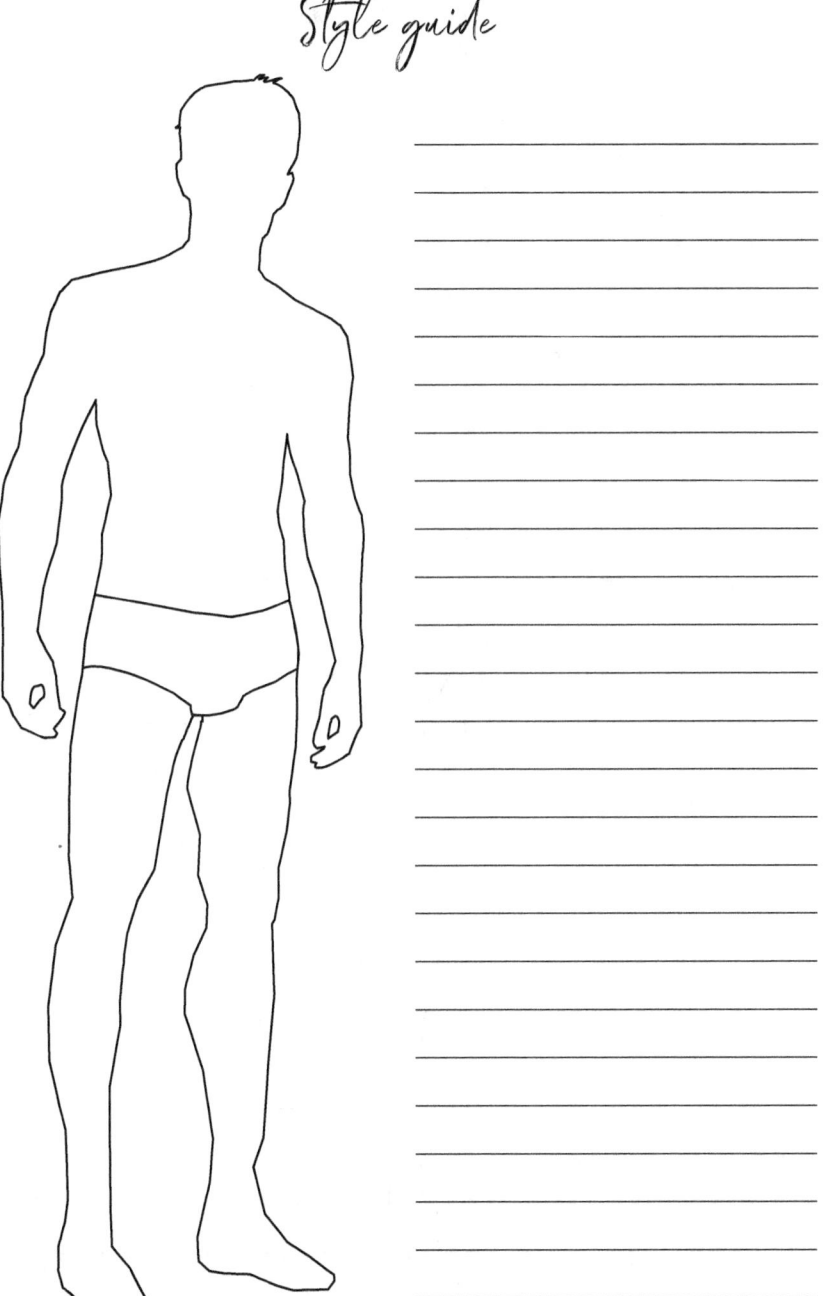

_____
_____
_____
_____
_____
_____
_____
_____
_____
_____
_____
_____
_____
_____
_____
_____
_____
_____
_____
_____
_____
_____
_____

FEMALE CHARACTER
Style guide

MALE CHARACTER
Style guide

FASHION
Vision board

FASHION
Vision board

CHARACTER NOTES

ACT III
Setting the stage

BUILD IT
Design your set

Characters are only half what they can be if they don't have a stage to perform on. The world you put your characters into needs to be well thought-out, believable, and have some form of logic to it. There are many factors to consider when building the world your characters will live and interact in. Write some initial thoughts here, then use the prompts on the following pages to organise your ideas about the world you would like to create. Go into as much detail as you can, but remember that not all the following categories may apply to your story. If this is the case, use the space for something else you'd like to explore.

_____
_____
_____
_____
_____
_____
_____
_____
_____
_____
_____
_____

Time or era: Is your story set in the past, present, or future? Will it alternate between past and present? Explore all your options and record your thoughts here.

Reality or fantasy: Does your story happen in the real world? On Earth? Or does it take place in a fantasy world or realm? Perhaps it's in outer space, or in a fictional world of your making? Is it a combination of both? Explore your options using the space below.

Place: Does your story take place in a city, a town, or the countryside? On Mars, or a fictional planet? There are many options to consider, so take some time to figure it all out.

Landscape and architecture: What do the buildings look like? Are they old-fashioned or futuristic? Classy or run-down? Does the architecture have a specific style, such as Gothic or modern? Describe the landscape your characters will need to negotiate.

Climate: Is it summer or winter? Autumn/fall or spring? Does it rain a lot? Is there a drought? All these sorts of factors will have an effect on your characters, their actions, and their surroundings, so take some time to write your thoughts here.

Magic system: Does your story contain magic? If the answer is yes, how does the magic system work?

Weapons: Do your characters need weapons? If so, what will they be? Keep in mind this will be affected by many other factors of your world-building.

Technology: Again, this will be affected by things such as time and place, and reality or fantasy. Consider what type of gadgets, if any, your characters will utilise. They can be anything from a fountain pen to a futuristic projection ring. If your story is set in the real world, but in the past, how far is it in the past? Do items such as mobile phones exist? Or are your characters communicating via letters and Morse code?

Transport: Consider whether your characters will drive cars, or fly planes, or ride in a horse and cart. Maybe you have an idea for your own transport invention. Write it here. Also consider how transport time will affect your plot.

_____
_____
_____
_____
_____
_____
_____
_____
_____
_____
_____
_____
_____
_____
_____
_____
_____
_____
_____
_____
_____
_____
_____
_____
_____
_____

Government: Describe the type of government within your story. Is it a democracy, monarchy, republic, or dictatorship? There are many types of government, so make sure to research thoroughly. Also ask yourself how the government will influence your characters' upbringing and their world around them.

Social hierarchy: Is there a specific social structure? Who are the people in power? Who is at the bottom of the ladder, and where do your characters fit?

Currency: Is there a financial system in place within your story? How do your characters pay for goods and services? Does the social hierarchy allow for paid jobs, or is there a barter system in place? Does your currency have a special name?

Language: Are there any languages spoken in your story other than English? What are the nationalities of your main characters? Do they have unique ways of speaking? Do your characters use slang, or a specific dialect?

Fashions: You may have already brainstormed ideas for fashion using the **Dress them: Style your characters** section on page 67, but if you have any further ideas, write them here. Don't forget to consider how other aspects of your world-building will affect what your characters wear.

Rules: Are there any specific rules your world will be governed by? Do you have magical creatures that do certain things? Or does your protagonist have a set of stringent beliefs such as not eating red meat? The rules you create can be anything you wish, but they must be consistent and work within your story world. Use this page to explore the details.

DRESS REHEARSAL

The final run-through

DETAIL IT
Outline your scenes or chapters

By now you should have enough information to start outlining your story in more detail. Use the following pages to write a few paragraphs that summarise each of your scenes or chapters. If you would rather get stuck into writing your draft first, use the space to summarise your chapters as you go. This will not only help you keep track of key events as your story progresses, but will serve as an outline once your draft is finished.

Chapter/scene: _____

_____
_____
_____
_____
_____
_____
_____
_____
_____
_____
_____
_____
_____
_____
_____
_____
_____

Chapter/scene:

Chapter/scene:

Chapter/scene: _____

_____
_____
_____
_____
_____
_____
_____
_____
_____
_____
_____
_____
_____
_____

Chapter/scene: _____

_____
_____
_____
_____
_____
_____
_____
_____
_____
_____
_____
_____
_____
_____
_____

Chapter/scene: _____

Chapter/scene: _____

Chapter/scene: _____

_____
_____
_____
_____
_____
_____
_____
_____
_____
_____
_____
_____
_____
_____
_____

Chapter/scene: _____

_____
_____
_____
_____
_____
_____
_____
_____
_____
_____
_____
_____
_____
_____
_____
_____

Chapter/scene: _____

_____
_____
_____
_____
_____
_____
_____
_____
_____
_____
_____
_____
_____
_____
_____
_____

Chapter/scene: _____

_____
_____
_____
_____
_____
_____
_____
_____
_____
_____
_____
_____
_____
_____
_____

Chapter/scene: _____

_____
_____
_____
_____
_____
_____
_____
_____
_____
_____
_____
_____
_____
_____
_____

Chapter/scene: _____

_____
_____
_____
_____
_____
_____
_____
_____
_____
_____
_____
_____
_____
_____
_____

Chapter/scene: _____

_____
_____
_____
_____
_____
_____
_____
_____
_____
_____
_____
_____
_____
_____
_____
_____

Chapter/scene: _____

_____
_____
_____
_____
_____
_____
_____
_____
_____
_____
_____
_____
_____
_____
_____
_____

Chapter/scene: _____

_____
_____
_____
_____
_____
_____
_____
_____
_____
_____
_____
_____
_____
_____
_____

Chapter/scene: _____

_____
_____
_____
_____
_____
_____
_____
_____
_____
_____
_____
_____
_____
_____
_____

Chapter/scene: _____

_____
_____
_____
_____
_____
_____
_____
_____
_____
_____
_____
_____
_____
_____
_____
_____
_____
_____

Chapter/scene: _____

_____
_____
_____
_____
_____
_____
_____
_____
_____
_____
_____
_____
_____
_____
_____
_____

Chapter/scene: _____

_____
_____
_____
_____
_____
_____
_____
_____
_____
_____
_____
_____
_____
_____
_____

Chapter/scene: _____

_____
_____
_____
_____
_____
_____
_____
_____
_____
_____
_____
_____
_____
_____
_____

Chapter/scene: _____

_____

_____

_____

_____

_____

_____

_____

_____

_____

_____

_____

_____

_____

Chapter/scene: _____

_____

_____

_____

_____

_____

_____

_____

_____

_____

_____

_____

_____

_____

Chapter/scene: _____

_____
_____
_____
_____
_____
_____
_____
_____
_____
_____
_____
_____
_____
_____

Chapter/scene: _____

_____
_____
_____
_____
_____
_____
_____
_____
_____
_____
_____
_____
_____
_____
_____

Chapter/scene: _____

_____
_____
_____
_____
_____
_____
_____
_____
_____
_____
_____
_____
_____
_____
_____
_____
_____

Chapter/scene: _____

_____
_____
_____
_____
_____
_____
_____
_____
_____
_____
_____
_____
_____
_____
_____
_____

Chapter/scene: _____

Chapter/scene: _____

Chapter/scene: _____

_____
_____
_____
_____
_____
_____
_____
_____
_____
_____
_____
_____
_____
_____
_____

Chapter/scene: _____

_____
_____
_____
_____
_____
_____
_____
_____
_____
_____
_____
_____
_____
_____
_____

Chapter/scene: _____

_____
_____
_____
_____
_____
_____
_____
_____
_____
_____
_____
_____
_____
_____

Chapter/scene: _____

_____
_____
_____
_____
_____
_____
_____
_____
_____
_____
_____
_____
_____
_____

Chapter/scene: _____

_____
_____
_____
_____
_____
_____
_____
_____
_____
_____
_____
_____
_____
_____
_____
_____
_____

Chapter/scene: _____

_____
_____
_____
_____
_____
_____
_____
_____
_____
_____
_____
_____
_____
_____
_____

Chapter/scene: _____

_____
_____
_____
_____
_____
_____
_____
_____
_____
_____
_____
_____
_____
_____
_____

Chapter/scene: _____

_____
_____
_____
_____
_____
_____
_____
_____
_____
_____
_____
_____
_____
_____
_____

Chapter/scene: _____

_____
_____
_____
_____
_____
_____
_____
_____
_____
_____
_____
_____
_____
_____
_____

Chapter/scene: _____

_____
_____
_____
_____
_____
_____
_____
_____
_____
_____
_____
_____
_____
_____
_____

Chapter/scene: _____

Chapter/scene: _____

Chapter/scene: _____

_____
_____
_____
_____
_____
_____
_____
_____
_____
_____
_____
_____
_____
_____
_____
_____
_____

Chapter/scene: _____

_____
_____
_____
_____
_____
_____
_____
_____
_____
_____
_____
_____
_____
_____
_____
_____

Chapter/scene: _____

_____

_____

_____

_____

_____

_____

_____

_____

_____

_____

_____

_____

_____

_____

Chapter/scene: _____

_____

_____

_____

_____

_____

_____

_____

_____

_____

_____

_____

_____

_____

_____

Chapter/scene: _____

_____
_____
_____
_____
_____
_____
_____
_____
_____
_____
_____
_____
_____
_____

Chapter/scene: _____

_____
_____
_____
_____
_____
_____
_____
_____
_____
_____
_____
_____
_____
_____

Chapter/scene: _____

_____
_____
_____
_____
_____
_____
_____
_____
_____
_____
_____
_____
_____
_____

Chapter/scene: _____

_____
_____
_____
_____
_____
_____
_____
_____
_____
_____
_____
_____
_____
_____
_____

DEVELOP IT
Further ideas

If you've made it this far then you deserve a huge pat on the back, a big hug, a glass of wine, a hot cup of tea, and whatever else you like to do to celebrate your victories. At this point, you should have a really strong foundation to build your story on, and you're well on your way to finishing it. If you feel you have more to add, use the following pages to write down anything else you'd like to elaborate on or come back to later. If you don't have any further thoughts at this time, that's okay. You can always come back and use this space if you need to once you've written your first draft.

THANK YOU

I would like to thank you for purchasing this copy of *A Novel Idea Workbook for Writers*. I hope it has helped you with the task of outlining and plotting your story, and made the challenge a little less daunting.

As an independent author, I rely on reviews and word of mouth to help promote my books. Whether you found this resource useful, or if it didn't live up to your expectations, please consider leaving a review at your place of purchase. If you would like to chat privately, you can email me at **kalast@kalastbooks.com.au**

Happy writing.

Scan the code to subscribe to K. A. Last's newsletter.

ABOUT THE AUTHOR

K. A. Last was born in Subiaco, Western Australia, and moved to Sydney when she was eight. Artistic and creative by nature, she studied Graphic Design and graduated with an Advanced Diploma. After marrying her high school sweetheart, she concentrated on her career before settling into family life. Blessed with a vivid imagination, K. A. Last began writing to let off creative steam, and fell in love with it. She is currently studying her Bachelor of Arts at Charles Sturt University, with a major in English, and minors in Children's Literature, Art History, and Visual Culture. She now resides in the countryside on the mid-north coast of NSW with her family and a menagerie of animals.

Website www.kalastbooks.com.au
Facebook www.facebook.com/KALastBooks
Instagram www.instagram.com/kalastbooks
Pinterest www.pinterest.com/kalast
Goodreads www.goodreads.com/KALast
Twitter www.twitter.com/KALastBooks

www.ingramcontent.com/pod-product-compliance
Lightning Source LLC
Chambersburg PA
CBHW071927290426
44110CB00013B/1508